Also by Sally

GW01048605

Just an Odd Job Girl
ISBN 978-1-9055997-12-3

Size Matters
ISBN 978-1-9055997-02-4

Just Food For Health
ISBN – 978-1-905597-23-9

Media Training – The manual
ISBN 978-1-905597-31-4

Sam,

A Shaggy Dog Story

by

Sally Cronin

Moyhill Publishing

First Published in 2013 by Moyhill Publishing.

A CIP catalogue record for this book is available from the British Library.

ISBN 978-1-905597-41-3

Printed in UK.

The papers used in this book were produced in an environmentally friendly way from sustainable forests.

Also available as an E-book
ISBN 978-1-905597-35-2

Moyhill Publishing,
Suite 471, 6 Slington House,
Rankine Rd., Basingstoke, RG24 8PH, UK

Dedicated to Sam
1 May 1998 to 11 September 2008

And, as always, love and thanks to David
for all his hard work in making books come alive.

To Ellen.
Thank you and
very best wishes
Sally Crown

October 2016.

Contents

1. In the Beginning

I was only three weeks old when I first met my mistress on an unusually warm Irish spring day in May. I was busy drinking milk at the time and barely lifted my head when I heard voices in the back yard where I had lived since I was born.

It was warm and comforting lying next to my two sisters as we snuggled close to my mother's fur and from time to time a gentle lick would lovingly dampen my fluffy coat.

I was already bigger than my sisters but my mother was determined that we should all be treated with the same care and attention as each other. She was an experienced mother and she knew how to raise strong and healthy babies. This would be her last litter and she lay quietly and contentedly in the straw lined kennel.

Full of milk and very sleepy, I sensed movement in front of our home and lifted my eyes blearily. I could just make out two very large shapes but was not afraid as the smell from one of them was familiar.

Since the day I was born I had been picked up daily and held high in the air whilst a deep voice rumbled into my small ears and a strong but unthreatening scent filled my nostrils. I have no idea what the voice was saying but it sounded kind and I had no fear of it.

I was also used to a smaller body with little hands that pulled at my fur and tickled my tummy. I loved these small hands and the chuckling sounds that the shape made as it played with me and my sisters.

This new being was different and despite my desire to fall asleep after my lunch, I pricked my ears up and turned my face in its direction.

I heard two voices making soft sounds and then felt myself lifted up in the air and held closely against warm and human-scented skin that was different from the smells I was used to.

I snuggled in against this scent and fell asleep hearing a soft voice saying a word that seemed to echo in my head. This was the first time that I heard my name and I have been called Sam ever since.

The days passed quickly and my sisters and I became more adventurous with lots of rough and tumble and nipping at heels and tails. We were allowed into the kitchen of the house occasionally and we spent more time with the little person with the sticky hands who chased and cuddled us as much as would let her. We soon learnt that there were certain behaviours that were not considered acceptable most of which involved teeth and making puddles on the kitchen floor.

My mother was content to let us roam around the house as she lay in a sunny patch of the yard where she rested away from her noisy and growing brood. We still pestered her for milk from time to time, even though we were now eating some small dried pellets as well. They tasted funny and we all still preferred lying side by side close to our mother whenever we could but I sensed that she was beginning to get impatient with us and would often stand up and move away.

I was getting used to my new name as my mother's master started using it whenever he came into the yard. One day I heard his deep laughter as his small daughter also called to me. I did not understand at the time but it seems Sam was the first word that she ever said, bypassing Dada and Mama in favour of her best friend. Trouble was she called my two sisters Sam too which must have been very confusing for them when they went to their new homes and were given different ones.

Anyway, back to my new mistress and her husband who had never seen me before. As soon as I heard my name I bounded over to the two of them and was made a wonderful fuss of. My new mistress picked me up and tucked me into her neck which I licked and savoured. I remembered her scent from her first visit but this time my eyes were open and I was able to look into her eyes as she gazed down at me.

"Hello Sam – you've grown so big." She looked over to the man and held me out to him.

"Here you go darling, meet Sam," she said passing me into his strong hands.

I looked up into a face with kind eyes and warm smile. I felt safe and secure high up off the ground and as they talked to each other my mistress stroked my head and back gently reminding me of the loving licks of my mother. I stayed happily being fussed over as the voices rumbled above and around me and almost dropped off to sleep but all too soon I was back on the ground and was soon involved in a rough and tumble game of tag with my sisters.

When I was eight weeks old my sister's and I were placed in a box with mesh over the front and taken away from our mother. As we left the backyard we cried out to her but she seemed to recognise that this was just a temporary separation and settled down into a patch of sunlight by the wall.

We were placed on a seat inside a bigger box that made a very loud noise and had too many smells to identify. I smelt my mother and also the man and child but there were also harsh scents that hurt my nose. My sisters and I huddled close together and shivered at the strangeness of it all, but thankfully within a short space of time the noise stopped and the man got out of his side of the box and came around and opened the door on our side. The movement as he carried us made us feel quite sick and we were pleased when we found ourselves on a floor looking out of the grating at several pairs of feet.

We also smelt dog smells and another smell that stirred up some instinctive sense of mischief. I edged towards the grating and looked through straight into the eyes of a large furry bundle in a cage opposite me. To my surprise it arched its back and hissed at me through the bars and I shot backwards landing on top of my smallest sister who nipped me on the ear.

After what seemed ages the man picked us up and we swayed into another room that had sharp pungent smells that tickled our nostrils. I sneezed and heard the man laugh as he opened the mesh door and took me out.

He held me firmly on a cold metallic surface that smelt sharp and acrid. I sneezed again and then felt a new pair of hands grasp me firmly and a strange object was placed against my chest.

A deep voice rumbled in my ears. "Sounds very good Patrick, he is a fine fellow, are you keeping him to show?"

"No, while I was away on a trip to the North a lady came to see him when he was only three weeks old, paid for him there and then and my wife promised she could have him."

There seemed to be disappointment in the man's voice but he was an honest man and had never cheated anyone in his life.

"Pity, I think he is going to be a very special dog when he is fully grown. He has a different look about him, almost as though he is listening to everything we are saying."

I was, actually, although I could not understand the words they were using, I was getting a handle on tone and emotion in voices and I sensed more than anything else what was being said.

However, these senses of mine went into overload as I felt something very sharp go into my skin at the back of my neck. Ouch, that hurt! And I turned round and nipped the hand holding me firmly across my chest.

"Ouch!" responded my master's voice and both men laughed as they examined the small puncture wounds in his hand.

"Yes, he is going to be a feisty one alright."

Despite the sore patch at the back of my neck I began to feel a little sleepy from all the excitement and as one by one my sisters were taken out and put on the table, I curled up at the back of the box and only woke when we were placed next to our mother in our kennel.

2. My New Home

That was to be the last time I would be with my mother and sisters as the next day my new mistress arrived to take me away. I was too excited at seeing and smelling her again to notice that we were leaving my family behind. I was a little afraid when I found myself on her lap in one of those large smelly boxes again, but this one seemed to be not quite so odorous or noisy and I found that if I tucked my nose up under my mistress's chin I felt safer.

It was a longer trip this time and I dropped off contentedly after a little while. I woke when I felt a strange vibration under the box as if we were travelling across a very rough surface. We stopped and the man I now knew to be my new master got out of the box and came around to open the door for us.

"Well Sam, you're home." The ground crunched under their feet and we moved towards a much bigger house than my home had been. The front door was opened and the man went in turning with a small box in his hand. A flashing light made me blink and then my mistress carried me across the threshold into my new life.

My new house was detached and stood in the middle of two acres of garden and wild meadow. I did not know it then but the grounds surrounding us would provide me with not only a wonderful place to play and explore but also would be where I met my first and best friend.

My new home.

At first I was in awe of the wide spaces that made up the inside of my new home. Shiny lino floors in the kitchen and wooden floors throughout the rest of the house made it tricky to keep one's feet and us Collies are not known for our ability to accept slippery surfaces underfoot. Some say we are too bright for our own good and this is apparently obvious when you consider our reluctance to trust in anything new, be it surroundings or food.

Up to this point I had enjoyed 24-hour milk on tap and because I was a growing boy and hungry all the time, had tolerated the hard and rather tasteless pebbles that my old master had served up three times a day for my sisters and me. Because Ireland is a little wet, an understatement I can tell you, our food was served in three small dishes under a plank laid across two oil cans. This kept the food dry and our heads as well when we ate.

My old master had given my new family a packet of the pebbles so that I could stay on the same food and not get an upset tummy.

Despite only being eight weeks old, I felt that perhaps it was time to establish my independence and although I was now hungry and missing both milk and my regular meal I declined the bowl of food that was put down in front of me and looked up at my new boss with a determined expression on my face.

This minor rebellion was to have long term affects and I can tell you in the next few days I was delighted to be offered all sorts of new and tasty treats in an effort to get me to eat. One of the main issues was that I did not like being out in the open when I ate. In my old home I was used to being under the plank which was enclosed and rather dark. Finally in desperation my mistress, who I had heard my master call Sally, put a dish of chicken breast and scented rice in a bowl in the fireplace. Of course there was no fire in the grate and the smell of the warm chicken enticed me to clamber up onto the tiles in front of the chimney breast and sample this latest offering.

It was definitely found to be more acceptable than the pebble dash and previous offerings and I was hungry enough to concede defeat.

After eating my meal, I backed out of the fireplace and turned around triumphantly to establish with my new family that this indeed was acceptable food for a Collie. Instead I was met with hysterical laughter and the sight of my new master and mistress rolling around on the floor. Unfortunately I was unable to see the funny side of this behaviour but there again I could not see my face which was now covered in soot.

There were a few other events that I did not find particularly amusing including Sally's persistence in putting me outside the back door, rain or shine immediately after I had eaten despite my being very tired and ready for a nap. It seemed to please her enormously if I had a wee-wee and she got ecstatic if I left a 'fragrant parcel' as she called it. There was much hugging and kissing before

I was finally allowed to retire to a warm spot in the house for a much needed rest.

I spent a great deal of time exploring the downstairs of my new home as at that time my legs were still too short to get up the stairs, but from the aromas that wafted down I felt that in time this area of my territory was going to provide a wonderful playground for me.

My own room in the house was the utility room and I must say my first night I felt rather scared and concerned. I was used to curling up with my mother and sisters at night, waking occasionally for a drink of warm milk or a wee outside in the yard. However, Sally had done a fair job of fitting out my new bedroom. There were layers of the local paper on the floor that stretched to the back door of the house. I had a fleecy blanket in the corner with some chewable toys and a rather lovely soft jumper that exuded her particularly comforting scent.

There was a lattice gate across the door into the kitchen where a dim light had been left on. I was warm enough but very lonely and for the first half hour I must admit that I did have a little cry to myself before falling into an exhausted sleep. It had been a very long and tiring day.

My mother trained me not to wee or do any other business in the straw where we lay so during my first night I was at a loss what to do when I woke up in the middle of the night.

I had no idea how long I would be there before Sally and my master David came down in the morning and I hoped that they were not the sort of people who liked a lie in.

Of course I could not tell the time but I do know that I tend to wake up at sunrise and go to sleep when it gets dark. It was mid-summer so the sun came up very early and I stood by the back door somehow knowing that I needed to get through it to a yard or somewhere where I could wee. Eventually I could hold on no longer and I am afraid that I wet the newspaper on the floor.

Just as I finished Sally appeared and viewed the pool in front of the back door.

"Never mind Sam, you have done very well and it is my fault for not getting up sooner."

Quite right, but very gracious anyway. With that she opened the back door and we had a very pleasant trot around the back garden and I thought I had better take the opportunity to complete my toiletry while I could.

The next morning I held on desperately and true to her word, Sally appeared just in the nick of time and I never wet in the house ever again.

Now a little bit about the garden. Of course at first Sally and David did not want to leave me outside on my own and as I had not had my last vaccinations I could not go out to meet other dogs. They had fenced off quite a large portion of the garden just outside the back door and this enabled me to be outside on my own in the warm summer sun. A couple of enterprising local schoolboys advertised a hand-made kennel service and when it arrived we discovered they had estimated my adult size rather generously! I never really liked it. But David spent an entire afternoon climbing in and out of the dog house trying to entice me in but I felt that like my food, I had to establish right from the start that I was not really a dog and would not be using this type of structure any time in the future.

Sally used to come out into the garden with me in the afternoons and there were two sun loungers and my favourite toys and my first baby paddling pool. Whilst she lay out in the rare Irish sunshine, I would sit in my pool and cool down. Instead of the kennel I would crawl under the sun lounger and snooze in the shade. It made for a very pleasant few weeks while we waited for my next set of jabs.

My new family had continued to experiment with various dog

David and I kennel training.

foods and fresh chicken and eventually we made an acceptable compromise. I even began to eat my meals away from the fireplace although I have to say that it was not until I was nearly eight years old that I tired of winding them up with my picky eating habits. Even today I have them very well trained and give credit where it

My first introduction to a sun lounger.

is due I am extremely well provided for. I was allowed full access to the rest of our home too and it was a great day when I managed to get upstairs all by myself.

Anyway, back to those first few weeks and some of the adventures that awaited me and the friends that I would meet.

Look Sally, I can do stairs now!

3. My First Real Friend

It may surprise you to know that I learnt to speak Cat before I fully understood human talk. When I was twelve weeks old Sally took me to the place with the strong smells again and I remembered the sharp pain that I had experienced last time and was ready on this occasion.

I did not understand the word that the man who gave me the sharp pain said when I sank my teeth into the soft part of his hand but it was very loud.

By this time I had learnt quite a few words as Sally and David talked to me all the time. At first I only got the basics like 'sit' and 'good boy' which always seemed to be accompanied by a small piece of chicken and because this treat was my favourite at the time I made a point of remembering these words as it obviously pleased her.

What I did not understand at the time was the conversation that Sally had with the man with the sharp object. He apparently told her that I would end up with a vocabulary of about fourteen to twenty words. How wrong can a man be?

However, on our return from this visit, to what I now know to be the vet, I was allowed a little more freedom and was introduced to the front garden of the house.

The previous owners had built the house in the middle of a two acre plot with nearly an acre of garden to the front, half that again at the back as garden then the remaining left as wild meadow.

The cultivated part of the property was laid out with hundreds of bushes and trees as the previous owners both belonged to families with garden centres who had obviously been very generous. The one drawback was the size of the lawns which required the hire of a local odd-jobber with a wonderful smelly monster that he rode up and down on and which belched regularly. One of my favourite games was slipping out of the front door unnoticed and barking encouragement to monster and driver as they drove slightly crookedly across the lawn.

It was a wonderful playground for a young dog but the reason I had not been allowed to play out there until now was because another dog was also using it as his territory. He would crawl under the flimsy fence whenever he felt like it and for months I thought his name was "That Bloody Danny" since that is what my mistress called him each time she saw him peeing on her begonias in front

My first swimming pool.

of the house. His name was actually just 'Danny' and he was a rather cheeky Spaniel who was a little lacking in manners, but more about him later.

There were also other creatures that used the gardens and meadow at the back of the house, such as foxes, feral cats and rabbits – all of whom might have been infected with disease. Hence my fenced off area by the kitchen door with my kennel, sunbeds and pool, affectionately known as Costa del Sam. Funny that I would end up living on the Costa del Sol when I was five years old.

Back to my new found freedom. I was due to have a final vaccination at about fourteen weeks but the vet said that I should be safe enough in the rest of the garden.

Sally and David had been living in the house for about a year when I arrived and I did not know that I was not the first four legged person on the premises.

One morning Sally left me outside the front door for a couple of minutes whilst she went back inside for one of my new balls to play with. The moment that she stepped through the doorway I heard a strange sound coming from around the side of the garage that was joined to the front of the house.

"Pssst." It was a sound that I was unfamiliar with and being young and foolish I immediately tottered towards the side of the house.

I poked my head around the corner and found myself nose to nose with a rather mucky, aromatic, white and ginger creature with one eye that seemed to move independently of the other.

I leapt in the air and shot backwards convinced that this very smelly individual was going to attack me.

"Calm down for goodness sake, otherwise she will be out here."

I got every other word of this because despite this creature's efforts to talk Dog he was disadvantaged by only having two or three teeth and he lisped rather badly.

"I've been waiting for you to be let out here, you've got it cushy, haven't you, in your little pad out the back?"

I was beginning to understand a little more of this garbled delivery and wondered how this strange creature had managed to learn to speak my language.

It was almost as if it read my mind because it turned around and waving a rather bedraggled ginger tail in the air he looked over his shoulder.

"I grew up around sheep dogs and learnt how to talk to them very early on." The creature strode off around the back of the house with me in tow, totally mesmerised.

As soon as it got to the back garden it turned and sat motioning with its head for me to do the same.

"She gave me the name of Henry, don't ask me why but as she saved my life it was the least I could allow her to do."

I was fascinated but at that moment Sally began calling from the front of the house and she sounded rather panicky.

"Sam, Sam where are you?"

Henry cocked his head in her direction and winked at me.

"Don't worry I will carry on with the story next time you are in your play pen. Off you go now before she gets hysterical."

I turned tail and raced around the side of the house and wagged my tail beseechingly at her.

"There you are, good boy, I was worried something had happened to you."

I desperately wanted to please her and when she picked me up I licked her face noting that she had just eaten something sweet and tasty.

After we had played 'roll around on your back and get your tummy rubbed' and 'chase the ball' Sally put me in my play area behind the house whilst she walked around the house with a large animal that made sucking noises. I had already demonstrated that I found the long cord attached to this monster rather biteable so she put me outside whilst she played with it herself.

I had only just settled myself down with one of my toys that I enjoyed impaling with my small teeth when a ginger and white blur leapt up onto one of the wooden posts of my enclosure and from there to the top of my useless but ornamental kennel.

Me and my lamb called Larry.

4. Henry's Story

O kay young'un," Henry grinned toothlessly. "Time for the next instalment."

With that he fell, rather than leapt arthritically down onto the grass and sauntered over to a sunbed that had just caught the first of the morning sun peeping over the house.

He lay down and stretched and I moved over closer for a good sniff.

Henry lay still whilst I examined nearly every inch of him. There was definitely a lifetime of smells on that cat and I could tell that grooming had not been his main focus recently, if ever.

Finally, satisfied that I would now know him anywhere, I settled down and looked at him expectantly.

"Happy now?" He sighed theatrically. "Did you want to hear my story or not?"

I nodded my head and rested it on my paws as I waited to hear this strange creature's tales.

The telling of this story took many days and, what I didn't realise at the time, was that our friendship did not go unnoticed. The kitchen window overlooked my play pen and neither of us saw the smiling face that looked down at us through the glass.

It would take too long to relate all the adventures that Henry experienced but I will try to give you an idea of how he became this bedraggled and toothless creature and one of my best friends.

Henry was about ten years old which is getting on for a feral cat. He had not begun life in the wild having been born, one of ten kittens, to a farm cat called Maisie. She was a great mouser

Henry does a spot of sunbathing.

by all accounts and this last litter was a surprise as she had not had one for over four years and the farmer thought she was too old.

Anyway, one by one his litter mates were either given away or sadly in one case taken by a fox. At last it was just him and his youngest sister that were left and the farmer felt that they would be a useful addition to the three other adult cats who patrolled the farmyard in search of mice and rats. There were two dogs that had been puppies when Henry was born and they had become friends over the years, hence his ability to speak Dog. Most young animals if brought up together will live happily side by side and apart from an instinctive and unspoken method of communication they will learn each other's language too.

Henry gave great service at the farm until he was about nine years old when the farmer died and the buildings and stock were sold off. The new owners were not going to farm and they knocked down the old barn and outbuildings and laid down concrete.

The other two cats drifted away as the mouse population decreased. The dogs had gone to the farmer's son miles away and the new owners brought in two large and mean looking Dobermans that could not speak Cat and only wanted to chase and eat him.

Henry soon realised that there was no job for him with the new people and reluctantly decided to leave the only home he had ever known.

With a last look over his shoulder he walked through the hedges, across fields and tried to find somewhere he could get food and shelter.

By the time he ended up in my large garden, Henry had travelled miles across the county, stopping at what working farms were left, catching a few mice here and there but usually forced to move on by younger and stronger cats on the premises.

He had to fight to eat on most occasions and eventually after several months he was tired, sick and hungry and decided to find himself a bush to go to sleep under. His intention was to let nature take its course which is often the way for animals, if allowed. He had endured enough and not ever having really bonded with humans he knew no other life. He had never sat on a warm lap and felt a kind hand or been given food instead of catching it himself.

The large garden with its hundreds of bushes and trees seemed a peaceful and unpopulated place in which to end his days and apart from the hunger that grabbed at his belly he lay down his head and closed his eyes.

My mistress, Sally, had been in the garden walking with a man that she hoped would come with his ride on mower and cut the acre and a half of grass a couple of times a month. She knew that with her new business she would also be unable to keep up with the weeding and was willing to pay someone else to do this onerous task.

She and the man were moving between some of the bushes to inspect the large privet hedge that separated them from the neighbours when she stopped and motioned the man to move back.

She knelt down and gently lifted a branch out of the way and was about to tell the man that she thought the cat was dead when she saw its chest moving up and down.

"He's come here to die." The old man from down the lane leant over her shoulder and shook his head.

"He won't last the night, better leave be and I will take him away when I come down tomorrow to mow the grass."

She looked sadly down at the dirty bundle of skin and bones and tears welled up in her eyes.

She could not bear to see any animal suffer and she could see that this cat had been through the wars and had probably had a very hard life.

After the man had gone, with a promise to return first thing in the morning, She went back inside the house and filled a shallow bowl with warm milk and crumbled a little bread into it. Returning to the cat under the bush she moved the dish as close as possible and carefully stretched out her hand to stroke the top of its head.

She felt a little movement beneath her fingers and continued to carefully stroke the dirty fur down to the tail. She saw the little black nostrils twitch and decided to leave the cat for a little while to see if it might be enticed by the milk.

An hour later she came back and found herself staring into two brown mottled eyes that were red rimmed as if the cat had been crying. As she leant forward to pick up the empty dish the animal moved backwards slightly in fear but gently she moved her hand around its side as it watched her carefully with its eyes.

Slowly she stroked the trembling animals matted fur until its head dropped onto its paws and she felt a slight vibration beneath her fingers. Satisfied that it would now accept her help, she placed another bowl with some newly acquired tinned kitten food in front of the cat. It would need very high nutrient packed food quickly if it was to recover enough to survive the night and, despite being just skin and bones, she had seen the glint of survival in its weary eyes.

Henry seemed lost for a minute or two as he stared into space as if reliving the dark days again when he was lost and so hungry. He turned his head and looked at me and then surprised me with some very interesting information about my mistress.

"You know young'un she can talk cat." He nodded his head a couple of times.

"At first I thought there was another cat nearby but the sound was definitely coming from her. The language was strange and a bit mixed up but I understood that she meant me no harm and I sensed she was trying to tell me I was safe."

Henry went on to tell me how he believed that Sally must have had a cat before and learnt to communicate when very young which is the best time to learn Cat and Dog language. She was a bit rusty but over the time he had lived in the garden they had often enjoyed conversations although he said it was a bit like a couple of foreigners trying to make themselves understood in a strange country.

Anyway, on with Henry's story of their original meeting.

Although the Irish summers are not known for either their consistency of sunshine or warm weather, that particular week of Henry's arrival, was dry and the earth retained the heat of the day. She had put down a bowl of water and some more food in the early evening and felt that the weather would not be a problem. She was, however, concerned about predators, as she had seen fox tracks and knew that there were rats and other cats that prowled the lanes and gardens.

She was also well aware that sometimes nature had to be allowed to take its course and felt that at least she had given the cat a fighting chance. Fingers crossed she went back into the house and waited for the morning.

The next day the cat was still in the same position but it was looking much brighter and somewhat expectant as it looked steadily at the bowls that she carried in her hands. She placed them on the ground in front of it and stretched out her fingers to touch the dirty coat. This time the cat did not move and she spent several minutes talking Cat softly to it and gently massaging its fur. Happy that he seemed more alert and was purring at her touch she left him to eat breakfast and rest in his sunny spot.

At this point I swear that Henry had tears in his eyes. He sniffed and tossed his head and glared at me.

"Don't say a word, do you hear?" He growled into my face and I shook my head vigorously.

After a moment he collected himself.

"That was a year ago, and I don't have to tell you that I recovered and have been living here ever since." He raised a paw delicately to his whiskers and then rubbed up behind his ear and down to his mouth.

"She feeds me every day and I let her stroke me from time to time as it obviously gives her pleasure, and of course I earn my keep because I can still give the odd mouse and rat a run for their money."

I was impressed and had a whole new opinion of my mistress. Instinctively I had adopted both Sally and David as my pack when I came into their den and she was making it quite clear that they were the leaders of the pack and I was number three. I wondered where that put Henry but I suspected that he was probably a lone wolf.

Henry stretched out on the sunbed and I paddled in my little pool before I joined him beneath the bed in the cool shade.

Both of us were unaware that Sally had come into the play pen until I felt the bed move above my head and over the edge saw two legs.

"Hi Henry, how are you doing you old moth-eaten love." She then made some rather strange noises that Henry responded to in kind.

This I had to see, and I squirmed out from under the bed to see Mr. Indifference rolling around on his back and purring so loud the bed vibrated.

I knew that Henry was not allowed into the house and when I saw how dirty he was I could understand why. As I watched this playful interaction between my mistress and my new friend I saw her hand go to the back of his neck with something between her fingers. A few drops of liquid fell onto his fur and I saw that she was wearing something that covered her hand. She gently massaged Henry's neck while he wriggled in delight and then she looked at me as I sat with my head cocked to one side.

"That should keep the fleas off him for another few weeks and you too my darling."

I was not sure what fleas were at that point but I jumped up and put my paws on her lap and laughed up into her face.

"Sometimes Sam, young as you are, I think you understand every word that I say."

She removed the covering on her hand and stroked the soft

Henry and I cooling off on a hot summer day.

inside of the top of my ear which I loved. My eyes closed in ecstasy as I surrendered to her touch. For me this was perfect, the leader of my pack paying me so much attention and a new best friend.

The three of us would often spend time outside in the summer months and as I grew older there was the welcome addition of a larger paddling pool to accommodate my rapid growth and Henry would take possession of the sun lounger whilst I would cool off in the water.

5. Henry's New Family

Henry would live with us for another two years and he had a wonderful life. When I was about a year old a wild black-and-white female cat who was only herself very young arrived in the garden.

By this time Henry was plump and healthy, although he still looked as though he had been dragged through the mud and a hedge backwards. His sense of smell was never very good and he would often ask me to give him the once over before he popped off to see his lady love even when I would tell him that a quick wash down in my pool might be advisable.

He was obviously, however, a smooth operator and within a few weeks we had a new family of three kittens living in the garden and Henry made sure that despite his lady friend's reluctance to go near the boisterous, year old, hairy monster I had become, his offspring were introduced early and became my friends too. This gave me even more opportunity to practice my Cat vocabulary and I actually became quite proficient.

His mate would keep her distance from my mistress too, despite Henry taking every opportunity to solicit massages and affection. However, when the kittens were about four weeks old they all developed eye infections, despite the fact that my mistress had begun supplementing their mother's milk with kitten food.

By this time Sally was working in the mornings at her business in the local town and she would get home about lunchtime. She never left me for more than three or four hours at a time and even though I am nearly ten now she still makes sure that I am never left for too long without company.

She arrived home this one day to find the three kittens on the doormat. Henry came over as usual to greet her and she could see his mate pacing back and forth on the grass by the side of the garage.

A little bemused by this turn of events she went over to the kittens and realised that all their eyes were gummed up with infection. She opened the door and went inside for a cardboard box and she scooped up the three hissing and spitting offspring and popped them inside.

In the meantime I was desperately waiting to be greeted. I was now very aware of my place in this loving home and I knew that

Mate… A little aftershave before your date please!

I was not supposed to leap up and down and shout loudly when either Sally or David came home. Instead we would go into the lounge to the 'greeting rug' where I would get hugs and a fuss made of me. I knew that the word hello meant a greeting and although I have no voice box I used to try and do my best to respond in kind.

Sally put the box down on the draining board in the kitchen and then came into the lounge where I was waiting impatiently. After this greeting ritual was finished we both went back into the kitchen and I sat and watched the proceedings with excited anticipation.

"Well Sammy – I think I am supposed to do something about these guys and their eyes," she smiled down at me.

She filled a small bowl with warm water and then tipped some fine white grains into it and stirred it with a spoon.

"Stay and watch your friends Sam, I'll be back in a moment."

She left the room and went upstairs to her bedroom and returned a few moments later with some fluffy white stuff in her fingers.

This went into the water in the dish and she gently picked up one of the kittens out of the box.

This was its first contact with a human. I had been introduced by Henry to the new family but had not been allowed to get too close. The kitten was not impressed by being separated from the warmth of its mother and chose to express this displeasure by hissing and trying to scratch Sally's hand. Despite this blatant display of ingratitude she gently squeezed the warm liquid across both its eyes and then wiped away the accumulated crusted infection.

She repeated this process with the other two kittens and finally satisfied that she had done as much as possible she took them out in the box to the garden and placed them next to Henry under the bush. She stroked his head and he licked her hand in thanks.

For the next three days the kittens were waiting on the mat when Sally came home. On the last day she saw the mother

Henry's wife and children.

deposit the third one on the mat before retiring to the bush where Henry waited. By this time the infection had nearly cleared from the young cats' eyes and the next day there was no sign of them.

Apart from Henry the family stayed away from all human contact and when the kittens had grown they left to find territories of their own. Henry and his mate lived happily without any further kittens for the next year until one day when my dear friend became ill. My mistress came home from work and Henry was on the doorstep. He crawled across to her and she picked him up into her arms. Although he had never been to the vet's she placed him on the front seat of her car and raced him to the surgery.

The vet told her that Henry only had three teeth left and was at least thirteen years old. A very good age for a domestic cat let alone one that had spent so many years running wild in a farmyard and the countryside. The good food and affection that Henry had received in the last few years had made a huge difference and I know from my friend that they had also been a very happy time spent with human contact for the first time, his friendship with me and his mate who had stayed with him despite their being no further kittens.

When my mistress returned I could tell that she was very sad. She greeted me on the rug as usual but there was an intensity to her hugs and her emotions that I had rarely seen. There was water coming from her eyes and it made me feel sad too. She was kneeling on the rug and I lay down and put my head across her knees. We sat there for several minutes as she fingered the fur behind my ears.

"He was so brave Sam," she began to talk as the tears dried.

"At the end he perked up and lay in my arms purring with his eyes wide open. I felt he was trying to say something but I felt the love in him and suddenly he was gone."

I did not understand death, as I had only known life and love with my pack and my assorted friends, but I understood her sadness and it made me sad too.

The next day the black and white cat was gone too as if she knew Henry would not be coming back. For many weeks I would patrol my territory and expect my old friend to pop out from under a bush and accompany me as I checked the long grass in the meadow or the hundreds of bushes and trees in the garden.

6. My Babies

I was not the only one who was sad at the loss of not only my old friend Henry but also his elusive and stand-offish mate. Sally decided that perhaps since I got on so well with cats that it might be an idea to have some house cats as a substitute. There was a cat sanctuary in the town and one afternoon, Sally duly arrived with a box and from inside came the unmistakable sounds of baby cats.

There were two "babies" as I came to know them, one mainly black with a white front and one mainly white with large black splotches. Sally refrained from naming them as she was more concerned that I would get on with them. Also being so little she did wonder how I would react to having cats actually in the house rather than in the garden.

I don't know if it was because I had loved my old friend Henry so much but it was love at first sight. I was only two years old myself and still a puppy at heart and the antics of these two newcomers gave me much joy. Sally was a little concerned at first as every time she picked up a kitten it was damp; however, she soon appreciated that it was simply my responsibility as a good dad kicking in. Cleanliness is very important as is making sure babies eat the right food.

Sally had brought back some specific high-nutrient kitten food to build them up but, like me, the babies were picky and decided

Proud dad to two new babies.

that my dinner was much more preferable. I was eating off a large plate at the time as I enjoyed pushing the bits I did not like off the edge and onto the floor. The second day my babies arrived they would join me on one side of the plate and gently help themselves whilst I ate from the other.

Sally had another concern and that was how I would react when my place on the sofa, next to her when we watched television, was invaded by the lively newcomers. No problem. We would all curl up together with Sally stroking us all in turn and we spent those first few evenings in dog and cat heaven.

This next part will break your heart as it broke mine.

On the fifth day one of the kittens started to be very ill and Sally was very concerned. I was left with one of the kittens whilst Sally dashed off in the car to the vets in the town to see what the problem might be. She was gone a very long time and I and my sole charge lay quietly by the front door ears pricked for the sound of her returning down the long drive.

Thanks Dad. Just off to find our milk now.

Eventually I could hear the sound of the engine in the lane and then the noise the wheels made on the gravel. I stood up with tail wagging as the kitten sat between my front legs. The door opened and I could sense Sally's sadness immediately. She had water on her face and she did not ask me to go onto the 'greeting mat' as we always did. She just knelt down and put her arms around my neck and whispered into my fur.

"I am so sorry Sam, the baby has gone, he was very sick". I did not understand all the words but I had seen my mistress in the same distressed state when Henry had died and I knew that I would not see the baby again.

We had a subdued evening and we huddled together on the sofa with the remaining kitten receiving loving licks and strokes. Over the next two days I took particular care of my baby but on the third day she started exhibiting the same symptoms as the first one. We were both devastated and I knew when Sally left with her in a box that this too was another goodbye.

I did not understand, of course, that my two new friends had contracted the disease in the sanctuary where they had been housed side-by-side with adult cats. The reasons were not important as I had been dealt a heavy blow and I wandered around the house with their small blanket in my mouth and kept whining at Sally as she tried to comfort me, often with water on her face.

She never tried to replace them. I think she realised that both of us could not stand losing any more friends.

Over the years we did, however, continue to make friends with feral cats, particularly at our home in the south of Spain where they were plentiful and despite the language barrier my 'Cat' vocabulary came in very useful.

7. Snow and Favourite Things

E nough depressing talk. Time to introduce you to some of my favourite things. The first of course is sausages. A delicacy that was not forthcoming as frequently as I would have liked but I have to say that over my lifetime this juicy addition to my diet ranked number one on my favourites list.

After sausages came cheese – any variety, but the smellier the better! In later years cheese would feature heavily in my repertoire

They don't come much bigger!

of party tricks and many visitors vied for the opportunity to see me in action.

The next two on the list are very cold. The first is ice cream and I first got a taste of this when I was about five months old, towards the end of my first summer. Sally and David were sitting in the car down at the beach and we had just had a great run and games on the sand. There was a colourful van parked next to the beach and a man was handing things out to a long line of people queuing up. David went off and came back after about ten minutes holding unusual smelling items in each hand. One went to Sally and they both started licking the object and making appreciative noises.

I am normally a very polite person and even back then had very good manners but it did not take long for the smell in my nostrils to send a message to my tongue that if this was very good for them to lick that perhaps I might join in on the experience. I indicated that this was the case by sticking my face as close to Sally's as I dare and licking my eyebrows. Thankfully she got the message and she took some of the white stuff on the tip of her finger and held it out to me.

I sniffed carefully for whilst it might have been good enough for them to eat I still like to illustrate the fact that I have ultimate control over what I deign to put in my mouth. Demonstration of willpower over, I wrapped my tongue around her finger and was first shocked at the ice coldness but then my taste buds went into overload as the creamy sweetness filled my mouth. This began a life-long love affair with ice-cream and whilst only indulged rarely remains one of my very favourite treats, right behind sausages and cheese.

The second cold experience was in my second winter, which had been as wet as ever. Sally used to despair sometimes as she placed yet another pile of wet towels into the washing machine and dryer. It was not only the towels needed when I returned from a walk in the rain but the towels from the back of the car and those that had to be placed on the sofa to accommodate my damp fur for the rest of the day.

However, one morning was particularly dark and threatening and was also very chilly. I of course had my own fur coat and was largely indifferent to cold weather but even I thought it a bit rash to tackle the beach this particular morning.

Suddenly when we were half way through our usual walk, large white pieces of fluff began falling from the sky. They landed on my nose and made me sneeze and when I used my tongue to remove them they were cold and reminded me of the feel if not the taste of ice-cream. Since I had accomplished my essential business – the delivery of a 'fragrant parcel' – it was decided to return home as more and more of the white stuff was falling and beginning to settle on the sand.

We got back to the car and drove home much slower than normal as even I could tell that the road in front was a completely different colour to normal.

Apart from a quick trip outside into the garden before bed, we all stayed tucked up in the house for the rest of the day. Sally and David did not seem concerned about the strange white stuff falling on our house and garden so I was curious but not frightened by the new experience.

But, oh boy, the next day was amazing. The sun was shining and when we opened the front door I was greeted by a thick carpet of white ice-cream with both cars covered from top to bottom with at least six inches of the stuff.

Sally had her rubber boots on and a thick coat and suddenly she and David were laughing and running around in the carpet of white. As usual I had to check this out cautiously and leaving two back legs inside on the mat. I stretched out and tested the white stuff first with my nose and then with my tongue.

OMG, ice-cream!

Cold but not immediately dangerous and if it was safe enough for Sally and David to be running around and throwing lumps of it at each other then it was good enough for me.

I charged out the door and found myself up to my belly in cold flakes – I joined in the shrieking and shouting and ran around my two owners barking and snapping at the white stuff. I stuck my nose down and ploughed up the long lawn leaving a furrow, then back again before rolling around on my back. Sally and David started piling the snow on top of me until just my head was showing and then ran away – I shook all the snow off me and raced after them and for the next half hour we played like young puppies getting soaked and exhausted in the process.

As the cars were buried we had to walk the lane that day and for me it was as if we had entered a strange wonderland where nothing looked familiar – it was exciting and one of those days that stays in your memory all your life.

While we are on the subject of snow, it brings to mind another favourite, but this is a time not an object. Christmas. Now I suspect that you are probably thinking that this time of year was my favourite because of all the food that was on offer as part of the seasonal celebrations. Not so. Actually, I loved the cards and the presents best.

Our mail in Ireland was left at the end of the drive, in a post-box attached to the gate, so I never had the luxury of attacking a postman or grabbing the mail as it came through the front door. I would wait until Sally or David arrived home from work and emptied the box as they opened the gate. Even as a puppy I had developed a little party trick that involved ripping apart any paper that happened to fall or be lying on the floor. To be clear, this did not always go down well with my owners, particularly if the paper was on the floor of the office and had only temporarily been situated on the carpet for storage purposes. There were a number of occasions when I heard Sally and David using words that were not part of my normal vocabulary when finding a particular pile of paper in shreds.

However, once I learnt that there were certain 'no go' areas, they both indulged my little foible by allowing me to gently remove the envelope from a piece of mail when they brought it into the house and provide the highly valuable security measure of shredding it to pieces therefore removing all traces of the address. As head of security this of course fell into my role specification and it also helped if there was a little advance on payment at the end of the job in hand.

Anyway, at Christmas the amount of post escalated and not only did this provide countless minutes of my time involved in the security aspect but it also gave me some wonderful sniffing experiences. Sally and David had lived all over the World and some of the hands and places the cards had been through gave them a very exotic aroma.

The excitement did not stop with the Christmas cards because there was also the tree. A large one that was placed in the bay window and decorated with all sorts of sparkling bits and pieces. The biggest draw for me however was that over the two or three weeks leading up to the special day, parcels, some of which were also very aromatic, appeared beneath the tree covered in lovely coloured paper, just ripe for ripping. For security reasons my owners' many gifts to me were not put under the tree until the morning of Christmas Day as they felt the tantalising smell of a dried pig's ear or smoked ham bone might have been far too much for me to resist.

Bliss! Not only did I get to rip the paper off my own presents but my owners very graciously let me rip the paper of theirs. I would

I can smell them from here – pig's ears in the blue wrapping paper.

lie, in heaven, as I became surrounded by a mound of shredded, brightly coloured paper and my job done I could then place my new bone between my front paws and begin my own celebrations.

This leads me onto some very special male bonding with David. Bones are very special to dogs and are very rarely shared with anyone else, even special pack members. But there is a slight problem, however, that occurs when you are halfway through eating said bone. It is difficult to hold between one's own paws and still get a good grip with one's teeth. When I was still a young dog, David lay down one day beside me and held the bone for me, between my front paws, upright and exposed for further chewing. I took advantage and this simple action became one of those pleasures that no day would be complete without. I have spent many happy hours lying on the floor with David and occasionally, if I was desperate, with Sally beside me holding my bone for me

Sharing my bone with David.

to enjoy to the full. I sometimes needed to remind them of their duty by standing in front of them, half eaten bone in mouth and an encouraging look in my eye, but usually they volunteered and took pleasure from it too.

There were many things in my life that made my favourites list but it would be a very long book if I told you about them all. However, there is one favourite thing that I embraced from the moment I entered my new home until today. Where I bonded with David during the bone ceremony, I bonded with Sally in a different way.

That is with the '*love*'. When I was very small, Sally would lie on the carpet with me and I would curl up into her like a spoon with my head on her arm and go to sleep much as I had with my own mother before we were parted. I think that Sally instinctively knew that I would miss many things about my life with my mother and sisters and one of those would be the feeling of safety and warmth that comes when you have a full tummy and are sleepy.

At first she would lie down and pull me gently into her and stroke me until I dropped off to sleep but after a few weeks it became a

The "love"…

Who did you say was top dog?

This is how boys do the "love".

daily ritual to have a '*love in*' as she called it. Even though I am now a very large and old dog and Sally's knees are not as good as they used to be, there are still times that she will lie on the floor and I lie down beside her with her arm around me and it takes me back to those early days. It is those times when I feel the most contented, safe and loved and if I get a massage down my back and shoulders at the same time I am in heaven.

Of course boys have a different way of expressing the '*love*' and David and I spent many happy hours rolling around on the floor in play fights and sharing my marrow bones but we also had our quiet times and I like nothing better when David would rest his head on my back while I napped contentedly.

8. Language

My pack was made up of the alpha pair, Sally and David. As I have already mentioned both of them talked to me all the time and as well as words designed to let me know my role in the pack and behaviour expected from me, I began to understand the tone and meaning of many other words as well.

It is a common theory that animals do not understand human speech except for specific and relevant words such as sit, wait, down etc. This is a misconception because if you have been talked to continuously over a period of time you do begin to attach meaning and actions to certain words and sentences.

For example, it is no secret that dogs, and I have to include myself, are quite self-centred and are only really interested in what is in it for them or this case me.

At only a few months old I was beginning to isolate certain words that applied to my well-being, specifically the well-being of my stomach. For example, my favourite treats in the world, cheese and cooked sausages. The latter was an occasional addition to my training sessions and they were, Sally assured me, low fat and healthy enough for me to eat from time to time. Personally I could have eaten them every day but she assured me that I would soon grow tired of them. This was one of those rare times when

I felt that she perhaps did not understand my needs quite as much as I wanted her to.

Anyway, I would begin to listen to conversations between humans carefully to determine when I might be able to partake of my favourite foods. Even if I was in semi-sleep mode which, for the uninitiated, is flat out with eyes open but in a dream state, I could recognise the key words.

Let me demonstrate. "I thought that we might have **chicken** tonight with cauliflower and **cheese** sauce." Or perhaps; "I went for a **walk** at lunchtime and I saw that the butcher has begun making home-made **sausages**."

I think that you get the idea. Now, as I got older I learnt more vocabulary and I certainly knew more that the sixteen words the vet had predicted I would know eventually.

I knew the names of all my toys. When I was six months old Sally had bought me a football but it only took half an hour to puncture it. Although we now live thousands of miles away from my home in Ireland I still have that ball and some of the other toys I was given. Apart from **Ball** there is "**Santy**" (a rather portly plastic Santa Claus), **Squeaky** and **Precious**. The latter got its name after we all sat through the Lord of the Rings Trilogy and you have to lisp on the middle of the word.

At ten I now have a very extensive vocabulary including not only my favourite things that are important to me such as **Car**, **Walk, Play**, **Football**, and **Chase**, but words that also get me wound up like **Flies, Magpies, Gaston** (my next door neighbour here in Madrid, who is a large and stupid Pyrenean Mountain dog), and **Cats** (not the wild kind but domestic variety who are very arrogant and self-satisfied and ask to be chased).

I was only a few months old when I began to string words together and although I sometimes would get wildly excited over nothing in the last ten years I have really got into the whole conversational thing.

The old toys are the best.

Sally often whispers to David in an effort to avoid "a certain somebody", as she refers to me, getting any ideas but she still does not have enough respect for my hearing as she should do.

Apart from things in my life I also know the names of all the people too. The other day Sally mentioned Henry to David and I could tell from her voice that she still missed that smelly old boy.

Where do the years go?

I immediately went up to her and looked up to see if there was something else that she might say about my friend. She just looked at me, stroked my ears and said. "Where do the years go Sam?"

Good question!

But understanding of human words and emotions is only part of my ability because after a year of being bombarded with vocabulary an event occurred which ensured that I would be even more immersed in the human language.

David was offered a job in Madrid, Spain and it became too good an offer to turn down. Sally and David had often worked and lived abroad for their careers and had always moved homes and countries together. In seventeen years they had lived in England, America, Belgium and Ireland but this time there were other considerations to be taken into account.

They had only owned the house for a couple of years and would barely break even if they sold up now and also Sally had only just bought a business in the local town and was in the process of building up a successful dietary practice.

It was decided eventually that David would go to Madrid and that they would alternate visits every three weeks at the company's expense and Sally would find someone to look after me for these few days at a time.

It was a wrench for them both but at least Sally had me. Apart from when she was working in the mornings, she and I spent all our time together and, apart from an occasional night out with her girlfriends, I was her friend and confidante. She talked to me all the time and although I already had an extensive word base this immersion therapy gave me a great many more.

This is the time that I wanted to improve my ability to communicate back and the result was my first spoken word.

The three of us had already established a very effective method of communication using body language, eyes and tongue. Well I had, they continued to use the spoken word. For example, if you want a drink or some ice (perfect for cooling a dog down on the one scorching day in an Irish summer), you lick your lips and hold your mouth slightly open indicating extreme thirst.

Sally and I have to take care of each other.

If you particularly like a morsel of food and you want more then you lick up as far as you can to your eyebrows once or twice to demonstrate that this is delicious and further examples would be appreciated.

If you are desperate for a wee or other business you put your paws up onto the sofa between a person's legs and hold your face up close to theirs and stare them out. If this does not result in the desired affect then you whine deeply in your throat with a rising pitch at the end to indicate a question. "Do you think that I can hang on to this for ever and are you getting the message?"

If I was in the garden and wanted a game of chase, which was let's face it is most days, then a sharp but restrained nip on the back of the calf usually resulted in a thoroughly satisfying gallop through the bushes.

They enjoyed the game as well and knew that the more arm

waving and barking they did the more I liked it. It was standard pack practice and I was delighted that my instincts were so closely aligned to theirs.

However, as I grew older and was no longer a growing puppy some of the goodies that I had come to enjoy seemed to be reduced to the occasional treat. I have to admit to playing on the common collie predilection for pickiness when it comes to eating and I am one of the few breeds that can affect disdain when a perfectly good bowl of food is presented.

Give them their due they were fast learners and discovered that if I knew that I would be offered a small morsel of cheddar, I would eat all my dinner. All was well and good but the scarcity of the offerings made me contemplate another strategy.

As I have already mentioned I do not have a voice box and it is virtually impossible for me to annunciate human language but I learnt to give a very good impression.

The first word I learnt to say that was understood was '**more**' needless to say. I really had to concentrate and it usually involved several parts of my body. I would crease my forehead, lick my lips, wag my tail and from deep in my chest produce the sound of '**mawgh**'. As you can imagine this became one of my party pieces and when David and Sally had friends over for dinner on his visits home I managed to obtain several pieces of after dinner cheese from all the guests who felt very honoured that I spoke to them personally.

I have to say that eight years on and I have had to modify this particular word as with any middle aged dog my waistline has expanded somewhat. This is also due to having my teeth cleaned by the vet three years ago... but more about dentistry later.

Back to '**more**'. About a year ago I was particularly intent of achieving a further portion of my favourite after dinner treat and I had been told three times to go away and find my bone.

Mawgh.

Usually I did this as I am well aware of pack etiquette and one does not want to push the alpha female too far as she is very good at the 'hot tongue, and cold shoulder routine' that reminds you of where you are in the pack.

On this occasion she was involved in a television programme and her directives to move away were slightly more offhand than usual so I pushed my luck.

The result was a frosty look to encourage me to mind my manners and a gentle sweep of her arm that indicated that I should move away. I do wish she had not watched so many episodes of the Dog Whisperer, that woman has a lot to answer for. Anyway, I ignored the instructions and she turned to me and looked my right in the eyes.

"You are beginning to sound like Oliver Twist and if you don't stop pestering me I will call you Oliver in future."

She obviously considered this Oliver chap to be quite something if she was willing to call me his name.

I scrunched up my forehead and really concentrated. I licked my eyebrows and wagged my tail vigorously.

"Oh, Ee, Va"

"Pardon." I had certainly got her attention now.

"ORH, EE, VA." I emphasised.

David who had been trying to watch the programme throughout this exchange turned the volume down on the remote control.

"Did he just say Oliver?"

Right on brother! And they were so impressed it resulted in an extra treat, my favourite next to cheese, a hard-boiled egg.

I now no longer bother with the short but ineffective 'more' and get right to the point with 'Oliver' after my dinner.

I also developed another word that stemmed for an everyday activity. I have already told you about the 'greeting rug' which is used to have a pack greeting when we have been apart.

David and Sally would always use a word over and over when we hugged and stroked each other and it was 'hello'. One day when I was about six years old, I felt the need to reciprocate and began responding with my own version which sounds somewhat like **'hayyo'**. Sometimes it comes out better than others depending on my level of concentration and I do get a real charge from uttering this word when we meet people on our travels.

There was one particular occasion when we were staying in our apartment on the Costa', where you find a lot of people who talk like David and Sally, unlike here in Madrid where I cannot understand a word people are saying.

We were out for their morning walk which they insist on taking rain or shine and this couple were coming towards us arm in arm. As they reached us the woman stopped and greeted us.

"Hello, what a beautiful dog."

"Heyoo." I greeted her back wagging my tail. Just as well she was hanging onto her husband's arm, to say that she jumped two feet off the ground is a bit of an exaggeration but you get my drift.

"Did he just say what I think he did." She looked at me awestruck.

"Sam, say hello nicely to the lady," Sally prompted.

"Heyoo." I uttered again and was rewarded with much petting and admiration.

This has inspired me to try and use other words, not all are successful but it is a work in progress and combined with my other effective methods of communication, I feel that I probably do better than most dogs in achieving the right balance of food and comfort.

9. Other Pack Members

I considered Henry to be part of our pack despite the fact that he was cat. I also included Danny, the dog next door, despite Sally trying to keep us apart.

Danny came to his new home and was allowed a level of freedom that is common in rural areas. He did not go for organised walks but was allowed to roam his two acres and the lane from a very early age.

These made him far more street-wise than I was and also gave him access to the other gardens in the lane, which did not necessarily make him very popular with the neighbours.

He would sneak in under the fence into our garden despite Sally spending vast sums of money "Danny proofing" our territory. She was afraid he would lead me astray and take me on one of his road trips. Whereas Danny was street-wise I was not and, being a sheep dog, Sally worried that I might get too interested in the flock at the end of the lane and get shot by the farmer. One night I did actually crawl under the fence at his invitation and found myself in the dark, on the wrong side of the hedge.

I think Danny was having a laugh at my expense and was trying to teach me a lesson for my previous cowardice in not following him on one of his escapades. He disappeared into the darkness and through the back door of his house leaving me stranded.

Sally who had only turned her back for a minute while she fetched a flashlight was frantically calling for me on our side of the hedge and I barked to let her know where I was and that I was scared.

She came up our long drive and marched down the neighbour's waving her torch and calling me. I had never experienced any form of mistreatment at her hands but I knew when she was not happy and that this was one of those occasions. I hid behind the dustbins and heard her ring the doorbell.

When it was answered by the next door neighbour I heard a number of words that I did not understand only catching a few.

"Your damn **dog** has been over into our **garden** again and this time he has brought **Sam** back with him and now I can't find him. Put your outside lights on so that I can find **Sam** and in future keep that **dog** of yours under control."

It was more the tone that alerted me to the fact that Sally was angry and that I needed to please her immediately. I slunk out of cover and up to her where she attached me to my lead and walked firmly and quickly up the neighbour's drive and into our own garden.

As we walked she only said two words repeatedly. "Bad Boy." And although I could not see it I knew that she was wagging her finger at me. Tail between my legs I walked beside her and into our own house. I was upset that she was upset and sat down and offered my paw in penance. With that she leant down and hugged me tight.

"Sam don't ever do that again, I was frantic with worry. I love you so much and couldn't bear to lose you."

Of course I did not understand all the words but I did appreciate the feelings that poured from her.

To this day I have never done anything like that again. I always know where both she and David are and even though I may not be on a lead I stay close enough at all times so that I can see them.

Luckily my lead is 26 feet in length which means that I get the best of both worlds, room to roam on our walks but still in touch with them both. We were very lucky to have such a beautiful sandy beach and dunes on our doorstep in Ireland that provided plenty of safe walking and playing adventures.

I have to say though that Danny still used to come through the fence and we would play together in the long grass of the meadow behind our house and I reckoned as long as I stayed on my side of the fence within sight of the house I could still enjoy the friendship of this freedom loving dog. He told me of his adventures but after a while I realised that the lane and his garden was his entire world where as I travelled many miles in the car with my pack and visited many different places.

Eventually he got bored and frustrated hearing my tales of the world beyond the lane and stopped coming to play.

David and Sally had broken away from their own packs to form their own many years ago. However, unlike in my case, older former pack members retain a high status in their offspring's circle and often visit. Siblings are also welcomed although I have to say that when all the packs come together for an annual reunion some of the younger members appear not to have learnt as much about pack protocol as I have.

Sorry, just an old dog talking and when I was younger I did enjoy the additional attention that I was given by small humans but I am afraid I have grown rather intolerant lately and tend to find one of my favourite sleeping places hidden around the house when we have younger visitors.

Apart from immediate pack members there were also visitors from other packs that became very important in my life during the time David was in Madrid.

10. Respect and Look After Your Elders

ally's mother was called Grand Mollie and I first met her
when I was about six months old. At that time I was really
only interested in my immediate needs but I stored away
her smell and knew that she was part of Sally's pack and therefore
part of mine.

The next time she came to visit was when I was a year old and
this time I took my new job as head of security very seriously and
guarded her at all times. I slept on the landing outside Sally and
David's room but during Grand Mollie's visit I camped outside
her door and escorted her to the bathroom during the night and
always preceded her down the stairs etc.

Sally had given me strict instructions that I was to look after
her and as her feet used to get very cold sometimes I took it upon
myself to lie over them whenever she sat down.

She was very appreciative and of course, whilst it had no bearing
on my devotion to her, the odd sneaked snippet of cheese and
sausage that she slipped me only confirmed that she was a worthy
member of the pack.

David's father lived in Dublin and he would visit us out in the
country. I went to his house once when I was still very young but
unfortunately his head of security "Tuffy" was not going to allow

Tuffy shows me who is the boss.

some 'wet behind the ears' new pack member have the run of her territory inside the house or outside in the garden.

She backed me into a corner, sat and glared at me, daring me to move. Even though I was only a few months old, I was considerably bigger than she was, but I felt little inclination to cross teeth with her and I never visited again. I know that she was just doing her job and in her way she taught me that you have to respect other peoples territory and that you must be prepared to drop the 'nice doggy' persona for a slightly more resolute stance from time to time.

I have never bitten anyone although I have to say I have been tempted from time to time, particularly at the vets. As I have got older I have become slightly less tolerant but have discovered that turning away and going and weeing as high up in a bush as possible is quite affective, particularly if confronted with one of the smaller breeds on a lead. If it is a larger dog and he is off the lead then I have determined that a dignified retreat to live and fight another day is by far the best approach.

When David went to Madrid to work, Sally set about finding someone who would love and care for me every six weeks when she went to Spain to visit him.

She had never put me in boarding kennels, knowing that I love company and would find it very lonely stuck in a box on my own for most of the day. I have to say that apart from a couple of special dogs I have never really been bothered about my own breed as I much prefer the interaction I have with humans.

There are two other humans who joined our pack and I came to love them very much. One was the wife of someone who worked with David and her name was Aunty Kay.

She was a soft spoken Irish woman who had a very gentle touch. At one of the final work parties that Sally and David attended before he moved to Spain, they had got into conversation with Kay and mentioned that Sally was going to try and go over to Madrid to see David every six weeks but that they were trying to find someone to look after me in her absence.

I think that I have already conveyed how very important I was within the pack and how much I was loved. As I mentioned, Sally had never felt comfortable with the notion of putting me behind bars for twenty-two hours of the day so that she could go off and have fun and so she wanted to find someone who had a garden and loved dogs as much as she did.

Aunty Kay immediately said that she would love to look after me and delightedly Sally arranged for Kay to come out to the house for lunch and to meet me.

The first time I smelled Kay I knew that she was kind and gentle and would love me very much. I sat by her all through lunch and when she seemed to understand that cheese was my favourite and gave me some, I also knew that we would get along just fine.

For the next two years I spent long weekends at Kay's home in Ballinteer and enjoyed expanding my territory to include large parklands and tree lined streets which as you know is every dog's kind of heaven. I met Kay's cats who after a little induction training left the house to me and retreated to the garden shed where they glared balefully at me whenever I was in the small back garden.

I also met Kay's pack members during my visits including her sister and family who lived abroad and came to visit.

On one of her sister's visits she went out one morning and did not return until the next day. When she did she had a very young and smelly human with her. I knew instinctively that it was a new puppy and that when it was being fed both it and its mother needed to be protected. I would lie across the mother's feet while she nursed the baby and would allow no one else near her at all. When the baby was asleep in its carrier I also guarded it to ensure that it was safe. That was my job in my pack, Head of Security, and even in young adulthood I was very aware of my responsibilities.

Kay also had a pack member who smelt of old age and warm musty smells. She wore a very long black dress and a black cloth on her head. When she first came I was a little scared, as all I could see was a face peering out from under the black cloth. However, her voice was gentle and fragile and with any old pack member you must be gentle as they do not like to play games as we youngsters do.

As part of my duties to my own pack elders, such as Grand Mollie, it was important to keep them warm and safe when they move around the house and gardens. I extended this courtesy to Aunty Kay's pack members as well and, at 96 years old, her aunt who had been a nun since she was twelve years old, certainly qualified. I rarely left her side and sat with my head on her lap as her hand gently stroked my fur.

They were happy days but Sally felt that Kay who refused any kind of payment for looking after me should not be put upon all the time and that perhaps we needed to find me another loving and caring foster mum to join the pack.

We advertised in the local paper.

My name is Sam and I am a Rough Collie.
My mistress has to go away from time to time and
I need a very kind family to look after me for weekends.
Must love dogs and have a garden.

We were inundated with offers to look after me and after Sally had checked through them all she decided that we should both go to people's homes and meet the applicants for an interview.

We conducted two interviews and after smelling the inside of the living room of the first one we both decided that perhaps being only a young dog I might be a little too frisky for the elderly couple. Also I have to admit there were one or two strange smells that I found rather overpowering including one came from a rather full ashtray and one from a basket containing clothes in the kitchen.

The second house was close by at a place called Bettystown and was the home of Aunty Katie. Like Kay she immediately realised how important I was and as I sat with my head on her lap she got the message straight away that a drink and a treat was required.

Sally liked her and her husband too and they lived very close to the beach where I walked twice a day. Katie not only loved dogs but was passionate about owls and the house was dedicated to them in all shapes and sizes.

I was truly pampered at Aunty Katy's house and was offered both the bedroom and a comfortable sofa to sleep on. I quickly communicated my needs, with my body-language and my verbal linguistic skills, and these were met with pleasing rapidity.

I loved both my foster mistresses and looked forward to my visits to them, leaping into the car and rushing into their homes to be greeted exuberantly which is the only way for pack members to greet each other.

I went to Katie's every other trip and so I had two wonderful foster homes where I was pampered and spoilt.

David came home to Ireland every six weeks and we had wonderful games in the garden while he was home. Sally and I lived on our own in the meantime and this is why I have such an ability to understand the spoken word. Some people may have thought her quite mad to hold conversations with a dog but I am a very good listener and she managed to avoid talking to me in public so it was our little secret.

11. Favourite Walks in Ireland

Let me explain first and foremost what a good walk is all about. Unlike humans, we dogs rely heavily on our sense of smell when we are out walking and you also have to understand that territory is everything to us.

For the first six weeks in my new home I was restricted to the garden of the house until I had received my final vaccinations against diseases that could harm me. It was important that I did not come in contact with other dogs, particularly those who might not have been vaccinated.

There are certain rules that need to be followed when staking out one's own territory and one of the most important is that one does not do any 'business' near one's bedding as this in not hygienic. I have met dogs in the last ten years who are confined to small spaces for long periods of time and they have no choice but to use the same space as their bathroom. They find this distressing and it stresses them.

I was lucky in as much as I had my own safe enclosed space in the garden that Henry and I shared from time to time with Sally, who used to lie on the sunbed with us. Later, I also had the whole two-acre garden to play in. However, apart from marking the boundaries of the garden with wee, which is acceptable, any other business had to be done in strategic places outside the boundaries to notify any other packs in the area that there was a new boy on the block.

From the first time I was allowed out of the garden, onto the lane that we lived on, I never pooped in my own territory again unless I was absolutely desperate or unwell. It simply is not done!

Anyway, during the time that I was restricted to the garden, Sally had been playing with me on a long lead. The leash was housed in a casing that extended to about twenty-six feet or could be shortened so that I walked by her side. This gave me the freedom to roam and sniff to my heart's content but when it was necessary I could be brought back safely.

We practiced these manoeuvres in the garden and when we finally went out into the lane I was already trained.

Although it was a narrow farm lane there was quite a bit of traffic at certain times of the day and Sally trained me to sit on the grass verge whenever we heard a car, allowing it to pass us safely.

I had been viewing and smelling the lane through the gate for a couple of weeks and was very excited by the prospect of enlarging

With my first harness and lead.

my territory. Apart from Henry I had not met any other animals and he had told me that there were several along the lane who were worth getting to know.

He warned me about two feral cats that tended to lie in wait for small rodents, and any careless birds that might land, and also about a dog who lived around two bends who was not right in the head. Apparently he had been hit by a car when he was a couple of years old and he now had a terrible temper.

To begin with, and because I only had short legs, we only went to the bottom of the lane towards the main road. The smells sent me into overdrive as we passed the five or six houses that lined the lane. Each had its own distinctive scent and inexperienced as I was I knew that there were different humans and animals within each of these territories.

The most fascinating smells came from the house that was nearly opposite ours and the people who lived there owned greyhounds. They used to breed them in my early days and at certain times a tantalizing aroma would waft into my territory and although I did not quite understand why, I would become very excited and boisterous.

When Sally saw that I was well behaved on the lead and was able to walk a little further we started getting into the car in the mornings and heading out to the beach which was about two miles away.

This was a wonderful adventure as there was a mixture of grass covered dunes and nearly four miles of wide sandy beach. Other owners would be out with their dogs and I was introduced to lots of new friends over the next five years. My favourite friend was a little white terrier called Abby who would see me from miles away and come rushing up to me. As I got bigger it got more difficult for her to reach my nose to kiss so she would have to jump up and down to get a good lick in. She would run in and out between my

Miles and miles of sand.

legs in excitement and try to get me to chase her. She was much faster than I was but I loved our games. I still miss her today.

I am afraid that I did continue to be very particular about food and drink even when out for a walk. I like many dogs believe that stagnant water can be harmful to you and this is why from a very early age I would always head for the side of the house where the garden hose was stored to be given a drink from a running tap. Of course Sally and David would often take advantage of the situation and begin to spray me with water which was slightly annoying but one of my favourite games was to snap at the spray as they swung the hose around getting thoroughly soaked in the process. Anyway, I am side-tracked again. When out for a walk of course there was no handy hose but Sally and David used to carry water bottles for their own use. It did not take me long to establish with gentle nudges and the use of the *"tongue hanging out side of mouth, obviously I am thirsty"* technique to train them both to let me drink from the bottles myself. For some reason they were reluctant to share with me, I cannot imagine why, so I ended up with my own bottle and at frequent intervals during my walks, especially in the heat of the Spanish sun I would keep myself hydrated.

I was really lucky that when we moved to Spain I would be able to enjoy the same sort of beach on the south coast and for me there is nothing like a walk by the sea with the feel of sand between your toes.

So in the mornings it was the beach and in the afternoons we would go out in the lane. Each week we would walk a little further until at six months old I could walk for an hour easily.

I was never afraid of being in new surroundings and did my best to leave my mark to let other users know who had visited. I considered the lane to be an extended part of my territory and as there were only one or two dogs who walked it regularly it became a competition as to who could mark the most. At that time I was

Still or sparkling?

still peeing like a girl and it was not until I was eighteen months old that I suddenly found myself cocking my leg in the air. This allowed me fantastic opportunities to pee higher and higher over other dogs' markings and I was confident that I was top dog in the area.

That was until the day that the mad dog on the second bend on the lane escaped from his garden and attacked us.

We were walking along minding our own business but I have to say that I found it hard to resist marking the hedge on the bend where the dog lived because he used to go wild and race up and down desperate to get out and show me who was boss. I had passed that way so many times that I was very blasé about the whole thing. After all, he had never got through the fence before and young and cocky as I was I enjoyed winding him up.

We had just passed the edge of his territory and had left him barking in our wake when we both heard the sound of wood cracking. We turned and looked behind us and were horrified to see a large black dog, with teeth bared, charging up the road at us.

I had been on an extended lead but Sally rushed towards me and shoved me between her legs and faced the oncoming dog. He ignored her and leapt on me trying to drag me out and under him. Sally was screaming at the top of her voice hoping that the owner would come out of the house that was a good fifty yards away but she could see that despite my thick fur I was going to be killed if she did nothing.

Sally would never harm any animal but she knew she had no choice and pushed the dog hard in the side. He yelped and moved away but decided that he was not going to give up. He leapt in the air and as he did, Sally grabbed him by the ruff and threw him into the ditch. I do not know where she got the strength but the dog obviously decided that this combined with the shouting and screaming that she was doing meant that she was a larger and more dominant dog than he was. Addled though his brain was he retreated back into the safety of his home and we ran past his territory to the safety of our own stretch of lane.

Shaking we went into our garden, locked the gate and retreated to the house. Sally knew the owner of the dog by sight and when she next saw him in the lane in his van, she stepped into the road and stopped him. She told him in no uncertain terms that she would report him and his dog unless he assured her that he would ensure that the dog was completely unable to get out of the garden again.

True to his word he reinforced the entire fence around his house and in fact a year later became our gardener and a good friend. He loved his dog despite him being vicious with strangers and other dogs and Sally understood how difficult it would have been for him to have the dog put down.

Despite the new security for the dog it was two years before I would even go past that corner, and I always stopped and turned around. Even when I was much older I would only go past the bend if David was with, us reckoning that as the Alpha male of our pack he would only pass if it was safe to do so.

I am happy to say that has really been the only time that I have found another dog to be simply vicious. As I have got older I have found that I am getting a little intolerant of uppity youngsters myself and in my own youth I was told off from time to time by older dogs who wanted to teach me some manners. It is true to say that their bark was worse than their bite and I am grateful to them for educating me about social graces.

As you can tell, apart from that one unfortunate experience I had a wonderful variety of walks each day and I knew every inch of them intimately. After five years all this changed and after spending at least half my life sopping wet I was to move to a very different territory with strange smells and hot sun and I will tell you more of that adventure later.

12. Car Rides

At first I was a bit apprehensive about the car rides because the first three times I was in one I had ended up at the vets' getting a large needle stuck in me. Every time I was put in the back seat I would start to salivate and felt sick. However, once we got into the morning habit of going to the beach I decided that if there was going to be so much fun at the end of the trip it was worth overcoming my original apprehension.

It is at this point that I must say a little something about Sally and cars. She is a bit of a petrol head and rather likes them fast and sporty. When I first arrived she was driving a BMW convertible which she had brought back from Belgium, where she and David had been living for two years. It was a left hand drive which made getting into and out of car parks a little awkward as you have to get in and out of the car to put the ticket into the machine at the barrier. However, I loved that car because when the roof was off I could sit in the back seat in my harness with my head back against the headrests and let the wind whip through my long coat. I can tell you that I was the envy of all the dogs that we passed on our way back and forth to the beach.

After about a year the BMW was changed in for a red Toyota Celica and I rather missed the soft top but there was a great central storage box between the two front seats where I could put my paws and watch all the action as we flashed down the country lanes. Because we spent so much time on the sand the back seat was covered with old towels and since of course it rains a lot in Ireland they soon became pretty damp. The car developed a wonderful, warm, soggy, doggy smell to it that Sally was always trying to eradicate with some form of magical spray or other. Personally, I found it rather interesting.

David belonged to the Mountain Runners Club and we used to travel around Ireland to their meets. I loved going to new places and sometimes we stayed overnight, which was also quite interesting as some places have very funny smells. I must admit to doing quite a bit of sleeping, stretched out on the back seat, but I always woke up in time to make sure we stopped regularly for sniffs for me and tea for Sally and David. I also had to mark every few miles or so to make sure we could find our way home again later.

Back seat driver!

After the Celica came the big Subaru Forester. Sally appeared back from one of her trips to Spain with this, in preparation for the long drive to our new home. I thought it was most comfortable but did need to establish early on that I did not travel in the back piece that was for luggage only and that I had would only consider riding in the back seat, directly behind the driving position.

The added bonus to travelling in all of the cars was the singing. Sally had always enjoyed a good tune and would sing along as we drove to the beach. After a few trips I decided to join in either humming or barking in time to the melody. We still do this today when we go out in the mornings to the mountain walk here in Spain and my repertoire is quite extensive. My favourite is 'How much is that doggie in the window' and 'Amazing Grace'. David made a recording once of our duet but unfortunately it never made the top ten.

Anyway the longest car journey that I ever made was from our home in Ireland to our new one in Madrid.

13. Moving to Spain

I have now lived in Spain for five years and it certainly could not be more different to Ireland.

Getting here was an adventure in itself. Sally had to make sure that I had all the necessary vaccinations and I had to endure a rather unpleasant trip to the vet to have a tracker inserted into my neck. I am afraid I have to admit that I find vets fair game and Sally always puts a muzzle on me when I am going to have a needle job. I am also extremely resistant to having my temperature taken as, unlike you humans, we have ours taken the 'other' end. It is neither dignified nor pleasant and I have found that sitting down firmly and glaring over the top of the muzzle is quite a deterrent, and many vets have simply estimated my temperature by feeling my forehead!

Another inconvenience was the stipulation that my clean bill of health had to be signed at the Ministry of Agriculture in Dublin, where Sally duly waited for two hours the morning before we left.

It was a hectic week as a large van with rough voiced men arrived and spent two days packing up the whole house to be taken to Spain.

We stayed the last night in a hotel on the main road and then headed out in Sally's new Spanish registered Subaru for the over 2,000 kilometre drive to Madrid.

I had been on the ferry to Holyhead before and slept in the car without problem. Once there we drove across England staying in a bed and breakfast for the night halfway across. I loved driving in the car and slept most of the time and I had the added bonus of marking different territories every time we stopped for a break or the night.

On the second night we stayed in a very posh hotel in Kent and because I was with Sally we were given a suite in the gatehouse which was very up-market and swish. Late that night Sally put me in the car and we drove to a railway station. I saw a man walking towards us across the car park and leapt around with excitement when I realised that it was David who was joining us for the drive through France and Spain.

The next day we arrived at the Eurotunnel terminal and queued up with other cars going across to France. The French police are stationed on the English side of the Channel and Sally and David handed over their passports and my papers which we had been told we absolutely needed for me to get into France and Spain.

Sally wound my window down in the back so that they could get a good look at my face too and after a cursory glance at their passports the two policemen started to interrogate me after calling for two more colleagues to join them.

"Eh, Henri, Philippe, come quickly, it is Lassie!"

Sally corrected them politely.

"His name is Sam."

"Oh, you are a beauty, what a bien doggie, you have a lovely 'oliday."

Even with my extraordinary language skills I found it rather difficult to follow the ensuing conversation but I found their appreciation of my handsomeness very satisfying.

Sally decided that the people in the queue behind us were perhaps not quite as tolerant of the delay as we were.

"Say goodbye Sam." With that a chorus of "au revoir Sam" issued from the control booth and I barked back much to the delight of the gendarmes.

The trip through France was uneventful although I have to say I spent most of it napping in the back.

Sally had tried to find a dog-friendly hotel for our night in France and had managed to find a beautiful and palatial chateau for us to stay in. I have a very good nose but you can't beat Sally's when it comes to sniffing out luxurious surroundings to stay in. David knows more about that than I do but he says he has a flexible friend, thankfully.

Again, because of my status, we were awarded a delightful room in what had been the stable block. This was, unfortunately, my first taste of marble floors and it took some coaxing to get me into the room in the first place where I scuttled across to a very expensive looking rug in the middle of the room. I have to say that marble floors are the one drawback of living on the continent as they are definitely not Collie friendly.

Anyway, the staff were very "Sam friendly" and the two liveried bell boys who had greeted us had mentioned that perhaps I might like steak for dinner. Unfortunately Sally declined what I thought was a very reasonable offer and told them that she had brought my food with her!

David and Sally went off to the main chateau for dinner leaving me with dried biscuits and a tin of meat and I have to admit to being just a tad disgruntled.

However, my moods are never long lived and I was just as excited to see them come back as I always am. I slept in palatial splendour at the end of their four poster bed with my blanket stretched across an antique silk rug.

We arrived at the border with Spain the next day and again Sally removed my important papers that I had to have to get into the country from her bag ready to show to the border guard. Passports at the ready we approached at the requisite snail's pace only to find that there was nobody there.

All that trouble to get me legal and able to travel and not once did anyone look at my papers!

Although that was the longest trip we made in the car I regularly travelled between Madrid and the Costa Del Sol which is about 650 kilometres. I have my favourite stopping places en route and in all over the years I must have travelled in excess of 50,000 miles in my life so far which is not bad for a rough collie from Duleek.

14. Nuestro Casas y Neuvos Amigos

ate in the afternoon of our second day of travel we arrived at my new home in Madrid. David had bought an old house in the mountains about twenty miles from the centre of the city. I had a large garden to play in and wonderful walks around this pleasant complex of 1960's summer houses and the added bonus was the number of lady dogs in residence who were open to some flirting and kisses through the fence on my nightly excursions with David.

The next year we acquired an apartment in the South of Spain and we would spend the winter months walking the beach and surrounding areas. David was now at home all the time and it was dog heaven. My pack was together every day and for the first time in my life the days passed without a drop of rain.

This is when my previous experience with Henry became very useful as in Spain there are many more feral cats than in Ireland.

In our local area on the Costa del Sol was a band of feral cats that spent their lives rummaging in the bins and catching rats and toads. At first, on our night time walks before bed they would keep their distance but Sally, who had taken pity on the skinny moggies, would take down dried cat-food pellets and roll them into the dark corners for the cats to chase and catch. She would talk "Cat" to

Sandy Spanish beach – and no rain!

them and despite the fact that we were in Spain, "Cat" appears to be an internationally recognised language.

This game developed to the point where we would be followed on these nighttime excursions by five or six black, stealthy figures. After about a year, some of the younger cats overcame their natural fear of humans and allowed themselves to be stroked and petted. One cat in particular stood out from the rest of the band.

She was a marmalade cat and had probably been the result of a union between a domestic male and a female feral cat. She seemed to have a litter of black kittens every three months or so and although Sally tried to catch her to be taken to the vet she refused to be picked up and put into a carrier. I did not quite understand why Sally wanted to take her but I heard the word 'vet' and assumed it involved needles of some sort.

Anyway, one of her offspring was a feisty little black thing, smaller than the other kittens who took an instant liking to me. By this time I was six years old and very well behaved and tolerant. At first she would come up close and we would stand nose to nose this tiny creature and I. Then she would leap high in the air and hiss at me as if she suddenly realised how big I was and what danger she might be in.

However, after a number of weeks, Mollie as we called her decided that I might be huge but I was a great asset. She knew that the other cats although unafraid of me by this point still kept their distance and by running in close to my legs she could get more of the rolling pellets without interference from the others.

Although she was Spanish, the basic cat language was the same and although she gave me fleas that took forever to get rid of, I hold her in great affection.

Now that I live in Madrid all year round I don't meet many cats, just the odd domesticated one who has the temerity to sleep on the sofa on the terrace without my permission. However, I have to say that despite reports to the contrary, dogs and cats can be friends and my friend Henry is often in my thoughts as I get older.

Apart from feral cats, Sally also enjoyed the company of feathered friends. Many of whom lived on our local lake in Madrid. Every day on our walks we would take corn or grain to feed them, particularly in the winter months, and gradually the ducks and one goose became less afraid of us. They began to eat out of Sally's hands whilst David kept me back slightly afraid that I might afford them treat status. On the contrary. My one delight was after they had all had a good feed was to make a quick pretend dash and watch them scatter back into the water. They and I both knew I was not going to catch them and the fact that they would wander up to me when chasing rolling corn, illustrated their disdain of my feeble efforts.

One bird, however, got a little too friendly with Sally for my liking. A goose whose mate had died adopted her and would fly across the lake from his roost to demand a cuddle and special feeding arrangements. He was a lot bigger than the ducks and I felt that I might bite off more than I could chew if I got hold of him so simply sat and glared at him from a safe distance. I won't go into detail of my thoughts about him but safe to say it was a good thing that David held me back!

I did gain two new pack members on our arrival in Spain and grew to love them dearly. Antonio had worked as gardener at the house for over 30 years and David had retained his services to look after everything for us too. He was a short, stocky man with a very strong guttural tone to his voice and he spoke no English. However, we learnt to communicate very quickly and Antonio soon found out that one of my favourite pastimes was to chase a water hose and to catch the spray in my mouth. Since the garden needed watering every day this provided an hour of fun for me that I really

That goose is dead – hold me back!

looked forward to. I think that Antonio enjoyed the game too as he would spray the bushes for a few minutes then turn the hose on me. I loved this game and soaking wet I would try to run into the house to tell Sally all about it. For some strange reason she did not see the funny side of it and would grab me and rub me down with one of my old towels as I tried to shake all the water out of my coat.

I used to follow Antonio all over the garden, including through the vegetable patch where he grew tomatoes and cucumbers, to make sure that all the work was carried out properly – he never shouted at me, although he might get a little irritated if I occasionally gave his leg a big hug just to let him know who was really the boss. Even though I am now at retirement age I still help him out every day and watch and wait for him to come through the gate.

My other pack member was Sinead who lived in Greece but who would come to our house in Madrid to look after me if Sally and David had to travel for work or holidays. Sally still did not want to put me in kennels so searched online for a pet sitter. We were very lucky to find Sinead who I fell in love with instantly. She looked after me several times and I knew and Sally felt that I was completely safe when she and David had to go away.

We made other friends near our house, and in the south, who would join our pack from time to time for something called Cava and Tequila. All I know is that Sally makes sure that there are plenty of my favourites on hand for me to eat during the evening, such as cheese and very handy snack sized sausages and special Spanish hams. The guests also help themselves to these delicacies but I don't mind as they are part of my pack too. I have to ask of course if I can have something off the plates, as just helping oneself is not polite, but I find that if I pass around all the guests in turn and say "more" they all are most obliging at sharing the treats around.

Usually after a very long dinner, and way past my bedtime, the

My new foster mum, Sinead.

music goes on and the dancing starts. At first I used to try and join in but it all became rather excitable so Sally now pops me up in her office behind a rather irritating wooden gate.

On the subject of music; my favourite singer is Shania Twain. Sally introduced me to her music when I was a young puppy. Here in our house in Spain whenever she puts one of her albums on I will rush up to the office from wherever I am and Sally and I do a little line dancing. I go in and out through her legs in time to the music

Getting ready for the Christmas party in Spain.

with a little barking in between. Great fun and it makes up for not being allowed to join in the pack dances.

However, I do have a party piece that I trot out every time we have guests in return for some small pieces of cheese. They have to ask who my favourite composer is and they run through the usual suspects such as Beethoven, Bach, and Wagner and then they say Shania Twain and I bark madly. Daft really, but cheese is cheese!

15. Teeth Cleaning

We had been in Madrid for about a year when one day I started to feel unwell. I had experienced tummy upsets periodically since I was about two years old. Sally would take me to the vet who would give me antibiotics and I would be alright again for a couple of months. At first they thought it was the food I was on and certain things did appear to be the trigger but no one came up with a definite answer.

The problem persisted in Madrid and in addition to the tummy upsets I began to feel feverish and suffered severe pain in my gut. We were going down south for a few weeks and the trip was agony for me. We had to stop every hour or so for me to get out and visit the bushes and by the time we got down to our apartment I did not feel very well at all.

Sally gave me some of my medicine and I spent a restless night. The next morning they had decided to take me to the vet where I was registered and as we left the apartment they noticed that I was bleeding onto the tiles.

They rushed me over to the animal hospital immediately where I had to go through the usual indignities of temperature and the most agonising examination I have ever had.

I also had what they call an ultra-sound, which looks into your body, and the vet came back very concerned.

Apparently since I became adult I had suffered from a swollen and enlarge prostate that was badly infected. There was only one answer and that involved an operation.

Before I had the operation I had to have pills for six weeks: antibiotics plus another to lower my testosterone levels. David and Sally decided to bring me back to Madrid to my normal vet, a very nice Spanish lady who smelt good and always gave me cheese after my injections.

I had no idea what the medication was for but I can tell you after two weeks something very strange began to happen. I lost interest in my girlfriends. Normally I would drag David around every night for nearly an hour visiting them all, kissing them through the fence and promising all of them my undivided love and attention. Now I would get about 100 yards down the road and wonder what I was doing there. Instead of thirty strategic wees along the way, I was down to one that lasted forty seconds on the nearest available bush. Very strange and I felt rather depressed about the whole thing.

Six weeks later and I could not even remember all my girlfriends' names and seemed to spend my time dreaming of my favourite foods instead.

At least the pain was better and after six weeks David and Sally took me to my vet's for the operation. Sally was very tearful which I did not understand as she told me I was just going to have my teeth cleaned. The vet gave me a little injection that I barely felt and I suddenly found myself feeling dizzy and sleepy. I slowly slid to the ground and lowered my head onto my paws. I heard David and Sally leave and tried to call for them but the next minute I was gone.

When I woke up I was still very groggy and my mouth felt a little sore. While I had been asleep they had taken the opportunity to give me a quick scale and polish but what I could not understand was why my bum hurt too!

I am absolutely fine now and have not experienced any further

Why have I gone off the girls?

problems, although I have to say that I do miss the girls and occasionally when I am out on my walks I get a whiff of a scent in the air that makes my tail wag and a memory of past lady friends stirs in my mind.

Of course the downside is that dogs in my position tend to focus on other pleasures, particularly those of a culinary variety. I have found that ladies are not the only thing missing from my life as sausages and full fat cheese seem to have gone the same way.

Other areas of my life remain the same. I still perform an extremely important function within the pack and I have to say that there is no doubt that they could not do without me.

I am still head of security and I carry out such duties as warning off magpies who violate our airspace, helicopters that fly too low, the postman on his motor scooter who is not allowed through the gate and any domestic cats who might think they can make their beds on the sofa on the terrace.

One of my most important roles is barking up the shutters in the mornings after my walk and barking them down again at night. I receive a couple of pieces of cheese for this particular job as well as a great deal of praise.

The most important role, however, is as security consultant and back-up to Sally. I listen very carefully to her language and tone and if she raises her voice or indicates any form of over excitement then I immediately move into the back-up position and growl and bark accordingly. I am very protective of her and David has said it is my job to keep her safe at all costs. For this job I don't need payment in the form of food and instead I accept several hugs and kisses. I still get my 'love' in on the rug in front of the fireplace and David still manages to get down on the mat to hold my marrow-bone for me, which brings me great joy.

I am a very happy individual with simple needs. My dinners are wonderful with French dog biscuits, cooked chicken and chewy gizzards. Two or three times a week I have a hard-boiled egg and I really enjoy these best when they are still warm. Sally is always watching her weight, and mine I am afraid to say, but she still lets me have the occasional treat including one of her yoghurt covered rice cakes.

I am not up to spending hours chasing my ball in the garden but apart from my two big walks a day, David and I also check the perimeter of our property for intruders after lunch. I have several rather useful holes dug under bushes that need inspecting regularly and I still enjoy sneaking a crafty nip at an exposed leg from time to time.

If any of you dogs out there reading this story are having as good a life as I have then you are lucky indeed.

I now lie overlooking the mountains as the sun goes down – I can see across the valley to the hills on the other side and I can hear the dogs down there below me saying goodnight to each other. As I look back on my long and happy life and the friends that I have known and loved, I would not be anywhere else but here with my family.

Also by Sally Georgina Cronin

Just an Odd Job Girl

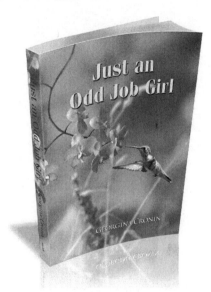

ISBN 978-1-905597-12-3
www.moyhill.com £6.99

Imogen was fifty!

She had been married to Peter for over twenty years and having brought up her children she was living in a wonderful house, with money and time to spare.

Suddenly, she finds herself "traded-in" for a younger model, a 'Fast-Tracker'. Completely devastated, she retreats to a small house on the edge of Epping Forest, where she indulges in binge eating and self-deprecation. Finally, when she can no longer fit into her clothes, and there seems to be no hope, she discovers a way forward.

Helped by a new friend, she rediscovers herself, making a journey to her past that enables her to move on to her future.

Size Matters

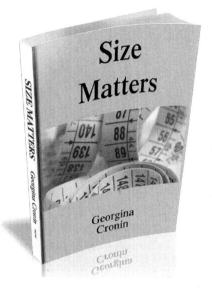

I wanted to find answers to explain how I had managed to eat and starve myself to 330 lbs.

This book is my story, but it is also the blueprint of the program that you will be following.

ISBN 978-1-9055997-02-4
www.moyhill.com £12.95

If any of these feels familiar
this book is definitely for you

- You can't take a bath because you can't get out again
- You don't even fit sideways into the shower
- You get desperate late at night when the chocolate shops are shut
- You are ashamed to take your clothes off in front of yourself
- You don't fit into airline seats and have to have a seat belt extension
- You struggle to get out of the car
- You can barely walk 10 minutes down the road
- You can't fit into public toilets
- People ask you when the baby is due
- You hate shop assistants coming into the too-small changing rooms
- You have stopped doing everything you once loved to do
- You have stopped sharing activities with the ones you love
- You are obsessed with where your next food is coming from
- You crave sweet foods
- You wish it would all go away

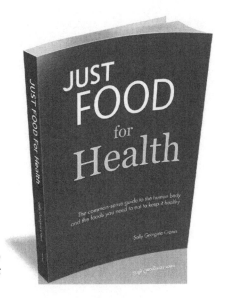

ISBN – 978-1-905597-23-9
www.moyhill.com £15.95

A new book from Nutrition & Lifestyle Coach Sally Georgina Cronin.

'*Just food for Health*'– a common sense guide to the body, and the foods we need to eat to keep it healthy: shows us how we can take the responsibility for our health and weight into our own hands.

Your body is your greatest asset, and is supposed to last an average lifetime of 70 to 80 years. Unfortunately, when it is fed on a diet that consists mainly of processed foods, the body is deprived of many of the essential nutrients that it needs if it is to remain healthy—not to mention the fact that processed foods are more expensive. The result of poor nutrition, for many, can be the development of lifestyle-related medical conditions including... high blood pressure, elevated cholesterol, diabetes, and excess weight.

'*Just Food for Health*' tells you 'How' your major organs and operating systems work and 'Why' you need the nutrient-packed natural foods to support and nourish it. It will show you how to design your own Healthy Eating Plan for Life, suitable for any age group, or for the most common health conditions.

Media Training: The Manual

ISBN 978-1-905597-31-4
www.moyhill.com £4.95

A quick reference manual for anyone who needs the deliver their message via "the Media", TV, Radio, Print.

It is rumoured that the art of communication has been lost but actually it has simply been adapted and expanded to suit the new technologies. However, we still use our voices and radio and television are very powerful tools that can enable us to reach hundreds or even thousands of people in the space of a few minutes.

Those few minutes can have an enormous impact. By reaching out and engaging with an audience you can increase sales, sell your latest book, raise more funds for your charity or inform the public about an event or important community issue.

This guide to media training is about opening the door to that opportunity and making the most of the experience.